AVERAGES

AVERAGES

By Jane Jonas Srivastava

Illustrated by Aliki

Thomas Y. Crowell Company New York

YOUNG MATH BOOKS

Edited by Dr. Max Beberman, Director of the Committee on
School Mathematics Projects, University of Illinois

BIGGER AND SMALLER
by Robert Froman

CIRCLES
by Mindel and Harry Sitomer

COMPUTERS
by Jane Jonas Srivastava

THE ELLIPSE
by Mannis Charosh

ESTIMATION
by Charles F. Linn

FRACTIONS ARE PARTS OF THINGS
by J. Richard Dennis

GRAPH GAMES
by Frédérique and Papy

LINES, SEGMENTS, POLYGONS
by Mindel and Harry Sitomer

LONG, SHORT, HIGH, LOW, THIN, WIDE
by James T. Fey

MATHEMATICAL GAMES FOR ONE OR TWO
by Mannis Charosh

ODDS AND EVENS
by Thomas C. O'Brien

PROBABILITY
by Charles F. Linn

RIGHT ANGLES: PAPER-FOLDING GEOMETRY
by Jo Phillips

RUBBER BANDS, BASEBALLS AND DOUGHNUTS:
A BOOK ABOUT TOPOLOGY
by Robert Froman

STRAIGHT LINES, PARALLEL LINES,
PERPENDICULAR LINES
by Mannis Charosh

WEIGHING & BALANCING
by Jane Jonas Srivastava

WHAT IS SYMMETRY?
by Mindel and Harry Sitomer

Edited by Dorothy Bloomfield, Mathematics Specialist,
Bank Street College of Education

AREA
by Jane Jonas Srivastava

AVERAGES
by Jane Jonas Srivastava

BASE FIVE
by David A. Adler

BUILDING TABLES ON TABLES:
A BOOK ABOUT MULTIPLICATION
by John V. Trivett

EXPLORING TRIANGLES:
PAPER-FOLDING GEOMETRY
by Jo Phillips

A GAME OF FUNCTIONS
by Robert Froman

LESS THAN NOTHING IS REALLY SOMETHING
by Robert Froman

MAPS, TRACKS, AND THE BRIDGES OF KONIGSBERG:
A BOOK ABOUT NETWORKS
by Michael Holt

MEASURE WITH METRIC
by Franklyn M. Branley

NUMBER IDEAS THROUGH PICTURES
by Mannis Charosh

SHADOW GEOMETRY
by Daphane Harwood Trivett

SPIRALS
by Mindel and Harry Sitomer

STATISTICS
by Jane Jonas Srivastava

3D, 2D, 1D
by David A. Adler

VENN DIAGRAMS
by Robert Froman

Library of Congress Cataloging in Publication Data: Srivastava, Jane Jonas. Averages.
SUMMARY: A simple explanation of averages, how they work and how they are used.
1. Average—Juv. lit. [1. Average. 2. Mathematics] I. Aliki. II. Title. QA115.S775 519.5'33 75-5927
ISBN 0-690-00742-6 ISBN 0-690-00743-4 (lib. bdg.)

1 2 3 4 5 6 7 8 9 10

AVERAGES

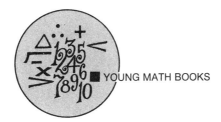 YOUNG MATH BOOKS

Do you eat the same things for breakfast as most of the children you know?

Do you have the same number of people in
your family as most of the children in your class?

Do you read the same kinds of stories as
most of your friends?

If you answered "yes" to these questions, then you eat an average breakfast, have an average-sized family, and make an average choice of stories.

An average is like an ambassador or a congressman. It represents a group. By studying it carefully, you can tell a lot about the group it represents.

The average is not the best from a group, nor the worst, but somewhere in between. Just where in between depends on the kind of average it is.

The three kinds of averages used most often are the mode, the median, and the arithmetic mean.

When the word "average" is used to mean usual or common, it is the MODE that is being used. If your father says he had an average day at work, he means he had a day very much like most other days.

5

Look at the questions on the first pages of this book. Do most of the children you know eat cereal for breakfast? Do most of your friends read animal stories? This "most of" kind of average is the mode. It is useful to know the mode because it tells about the largest part of a group.

What kinds of sandwiches do your friends like to eat for lunch? Which sandwich is the mode? Ask each friend to bring his favorite sandwich to school. Put the sandwiches in piles, starting a new pile for each different kind of sandwich. Which pile has the largest number of sandwiches? That is the mode.

Ask the children on your street to stand in groups according to their ages. Which age group has the most children? What is the modal age of children on your street?

Sometimes there is more than one mode.

Here is a picture of the children on my street. The group of six-year-olds has the same number of children as the group of eight-year-olds. These two groups are the largest. The children on my street have two modal ages: six years and eight years.

The MEDIAN is the second kind of average. The median is the middle of a group when it is arranged in an order, for example: from best to worst, lowest to highest, or youngest to oldest.

Can you think of other ways to arrange things in an order?

How would you arrange your crayons?

a pile of magazines?

a collection of racing cars?

Stand in line with four other children in order of height. If two children are the same height it doesn't matter who stands ahead of whom. Does it matter whether the line begins with the tallest child or the shortest child?

If you are in the line it may be hard to see who is in the middle. Drawing a picture will help you. Your picture may look like this:

The child who has the same number of children ahead of him as behind him is standing in the middle of the line. His height is the median for the group.

If your little brother comes and joins the line,

does the median change? There is no longer just one child in the middle of the line. Find the two children who are standing closest to the middle. The median height for the group is between their heights.

Make lines of coins or buttons. Order the coins by year or brightness. Order the buttons by size or the number of holes. Find the median for each line.

Make more lines with other things. Choose an order for each line, and find the median.

Can you tell ahead of time which lines will have one thing in the middle and which lines will have two things, one on each side of the middle? Here is a hint: count the number of things in each line before you look for the median.

Ask your friends to stand in a line according to age.

Ask them to stand in a line according to weight.

Ask them to stand in a line according to shoe size.

Does the same person always represent the median?

The median is an easy average to find. When things in a group are different—but not too different—from one another, the median is a good average to use.

The median pair of shoes is almost the same size as the rest. It gives you a fair idea of the group.

When things in a group are *very* different from one another, does the median still give a fair idea of the group?

Most of these shoes are either very big or very small—a very different size from the median. If you wanted to tell someone about the average size of these shoes, it would be fairer to tell about the mode.

The ARITHMETIC MEAN (pronounced ar-ith-MET-ic) is the third kind of average. It is found by doing arithmetic—by adding and dividing. The average you compute in school is usually the arithmetic mean.

The arithmetic mean can tell you the average height of children in a group or the average weight of fish in a basket. It tells you how tall each child would be if all children were the same height.

It tells you how many pounds each fish would weigh if all fish weighed the same amount.

Collect some pencils and lay them end to end in a straight line. They do not need to be in any particular order.

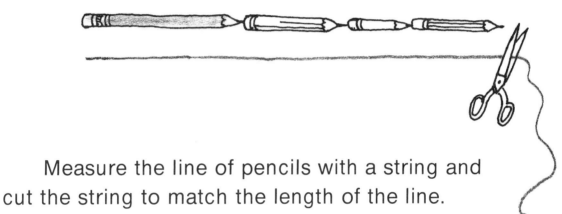

Measure the line of pencils with a string and cut the string to match the length of the line.

Fold the string. If you used four pencils, fold the string to make four equal lengths. If you used three pencils, fold the string to make three equal lengths.

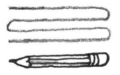

The length of the folded string is the mean length of the pencils. It shows you how long each pencil would be if all the pencils were the same length.

Get a box of crackers and take out a handful.
Ask each of your friends also to take out a
handful. If you do not have a box of crackers, you
can use a bag of cookies or a box of dry cereal.
Before you eat the crackers, find out how big the
average handful is.

Ask each friend to write down how many crackers he has, and then to put his crackers on a plate with yours.

Divide the crackers among yourselves so that everyone has the same number of crackers. If there are some left over, you can break them into pieces and share the pieces. If each of you now has 6 crackers, the mean handful is 6 crackers. If each of you has 6 crackers and a small piece, the mean handful is between 6 and 7 crackers.

Was your handful bigger or smaller than the mean? What about your friends'? Would the average handful of your friends be the same as the average handful of their parents?

Do you know the mean attendance in your class? Keep a record of the number of children who attend the class each day for a week, or 10 days, or even longer. Add the numbers you have recorded and then divide by the number of days that you kept the record. Your answer is the arithmetic mean of the attendance of the children in your class.

What do you think? Will the mean attendance change if you keep the record for a month rather than a week? Will it be different in the winter than in the spring?

You can also find the arithmetic mean for the amount of money you spend on candy each week, or for the number of minutes it takes you to make your bed each day.

The mode, the median, and the arithmetic mean are all found by counting.

What is the average number of animal stories your friends read each week? Which average will you use? The mode, the median, and the arithmetic mean may be different numbers.

Hmmmm.

More people read 2 stories, so that must be the _mode_.

3 is in the middle of 1,2,3,4,5, so that must be the _median_.

Seven of us read a total of 16 stories, so the _mean_ must be somewhere between 2 and 3. Closer to 2 I guess.

I think I'll try to find a good book about an average alligator who isn't too mean.

When mathematicians use the word "average," they tell you exactly what kind of average they are using. They are also very careful to say which group they are describing. Your friends may read an average of 3 animal stories each week, but school librarians may read an average of 8 animal stories each week.

Are you an average child?

You can count many things about yourself and find that in some ways you are average for some groups.

You can count other things about yourself
and find that you are not average for any group.
  Each of us is average in some ways. Each of
us is different from the average in other ways.
  Isn't that nice?

ABOUT THE AUTHOR

Jane Jonas Srivastava has been teaching mathematics since receiving her master's degree in education. She has worked in the University of Illinois Arithmetic Project in Watertown, Massachusetts, and in Simon Fraser University's project to initiate a new primary arithmetic program in local schools.

Mrs. Srivastava now spends much of her time looking after her two young children and baking bread for the family. Her husband is a professor of biological science at Simon Fraser University. They live in North Vancouver, British Columbia.

ABOUT THE ILLUSTRATOR

Aliki worked in many phases of the art field before she began illustrating and writing children's books. Now, when she is not too busy with books, she makes puppets and scenery for the family puppet theater, weaves baskets and macramés.

Aliki Brandenberg grew up in Philadelphia and graduated from the Museum College of Art. She has traveled to many countries with her husband, Franz Brandenberg, and their children, Jason and Alexa. They now live in New York City.